Gainsborough

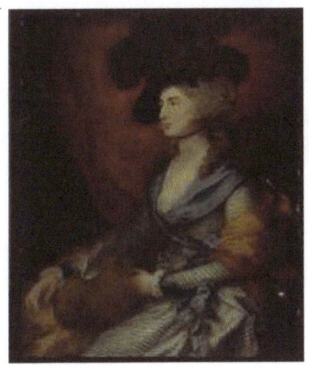

By Max Rothschild

**Illustrated With Eight
Reproductions In Colour**

MRS. SIDDONS.

This famous portrait of Mrs. Siddons was painted in 1784. It is one of the chief ornaments in the National Gallery, London. It represents the celebrated actress in her twenty-ninth year. The picture was purchased in 1862 from a relative of Mrs. Siddons.

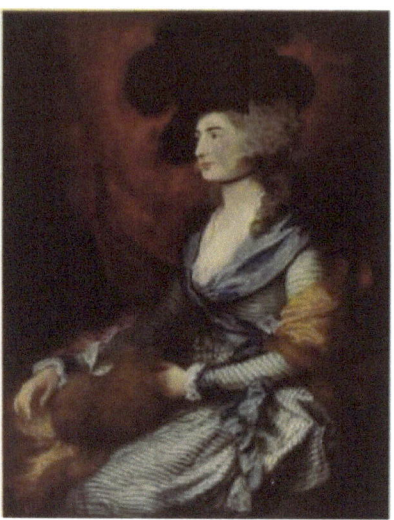

PLATE I.—MRS. SIDDONS.

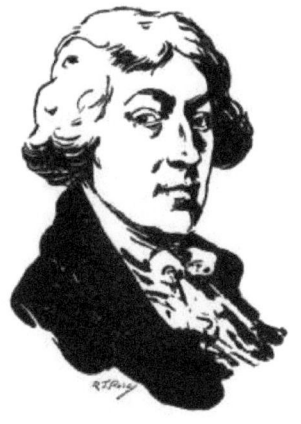

I

PAINTING IN ENGLAND BEFORE GAINSBOROUGH

THE British school of painting was, compared with those of the other nations of Western Europe, the latest to develop. In Italy, Spain, France, the Netherlands, Germany, and even Scandinavia painting and sculpture flourished as early as the Gothic Age, and in most of these countries the Renaissance produced a host of craftsmen whose works still endure among the most superb creations of artistic genius. It is now inexact to say that there was no *primitive* period in British Art; the thirteenth, fourteenth, and fifteenth centuries, so resplendent on the Continent with pictures and statues reflecting the character, the aspirations, the temperament of the respective peoples that produced them, produced works of art also in these islands. There are ample records of pictures having been painted in England, both religious subjects and portraits, at a very early age, as far back even as the reign of Henry III.; of such remote productions little has been preserved, but there are still extant a few specimens, from the thirteenth century onwards, as well as portraits of Henry VI., Henry VII., and effigies of princes and earls, which cause us to mourn the loss of a large number of paintings; they are at times grotesque and so thoroughly bad as to be a quite negligible quantity as works of art, though no doubt historically interesting.

PLATE II.—RALPH SCHOMBERG, M.D.

This canvas can be seen in the National Gallery, and represents a member of the family of Field-Marshal Duke Schomberg, who was killed in 1690 at the Battle of the Boyne. It is painted in the fashion of the time, a full figure in the open air, and is a very fine example of Gainsborough's work.

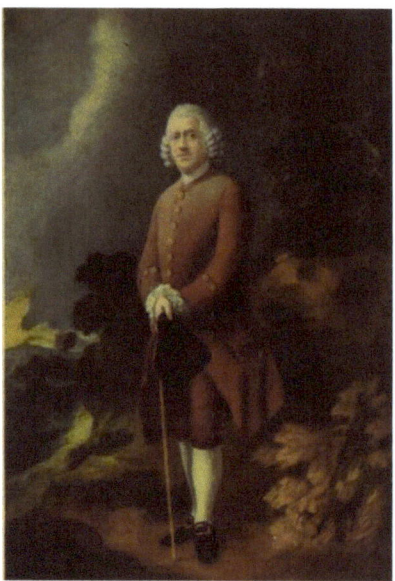

PLATE II.—RALPH SCHOMBERG, M.D.

It may be stated for our purposes that until the reign of Henry VIII. the art of painting was non-existent in England. This luxurious and liberal monarch it was who first gave any real and discerning encouragement to art, and the year 1526 must ever be memorable as the one in which was laid the foundation-stone of British Art. In that year the Earl of Arundel returned from a journey on the Continent; he was accompanied by a young man of powerful build, "with a swarthy sensual face, a neck like a bull, and an eye unlikely to endure contradiction." This was Hans Holbein, who was then thirty years of age, and whose fame had already been spread far and wide by the eloquent praises of Erasmus. Whether the monarch appreciated the depth and subtlety of the painter's genius better than did his own fellow-citizens of Basle, or whether his attitude towards him was prompted by a sense of vanity and ostentation is a question of little moment; the fact remains that he succeeded by his favour and a pension of two hundred florins in fixing the painter at the English court, and thus rendered an incomparable service to his country's art. With the exception of a few lengthy excursions abroad, Holbein lived continuously in England for twenty-eight years, until his death of the plague in 1543.

The art of Holbein, with all his genius, with all his success and popularity at court, does not seem to have taken root in England. The soil was not congenial, and when the plant withered no off-shoots remained behind; he formed no school in this country, had no pupils capable of carrying on his work, and continuing his tradition. With his death, the first short chapter in the history of art in Great Britain closes like a book, and for a time it looks as though the seeds sown by Henry VIII. were destined never to bear fruit. But one notable result had been attained; painting had gained a place in popular estimation, and succeeding sovereigns followed Henry's example in attracting to England talented artists from over seas. Thus Antonio Moro came for a brief period to the court of Mary; Lucas de Heere, Zucchero, and Van Somer to that of Queen Elizabeth. During this reign, for the first time, distinction is obtained by two artists of British birth, the miniature painters Hilliard and Oliver, but they again leave no very important followers (with the exception of the younger Oliver), and their isolated merit had no share in the formation of a native school.

With the accession of Charles the First art began to take a much more important position in the life of the nation. Charles was a man of considerable taste and refined discernment; no longer content with attracting artists to his court, he began to collect fine works purchased in other countries, his example being followed by his brother Prince Henry, by the Earl of Arundel and others among his courtiers; thus the works of the great Italians found their way into England. The walls of the royal palaces blazoned with the handiwork of Raphael and Leonardo da Vinci, Correggio and Veronese, Titian and Tintoretto; from the Netherlands came pictures by Rembrandt and Rubens, and the influx thus started was destined to continue until England became the greatest artistic store-house in the world.

The greatest artistic event of the reign of Charles I.—the most far-reaching, indeed, in the whole history of art in this country—was the coming of Van Dyck in 1632, for to his influence is directly due the birth and development of our native school of painting culminating in the golden period of the following century.

Van Dyck was thirty-three years of age when he came to England; his talent was at its highest point of perfection; he was almost immediately attached to the court among the royal painters, and his success was rapid and unequalled. The king and queen and their children sat to him again and again; there was no courtier or noble lady but wished her portrait to be painted by the fashionable and fascinating artist, and the habit of portrait-painting became so firmly established that neither the revolution, nor the Puritan régime, which followed the death of Charles I., were able to eradicate it.

Van Dyck's commissions were so numerous that it became impossible for him to execute the whole of them with his own hand; Van Dyck, as his master Rubens had done in Antwerp, filled his studio with assistants and pupils whom he trained, and who frequently painted the more unimportant portions of his portraits, such as draperies and background. In this manner a considerable number of men received tuition of the utmost value, and, though many of them were foreigners, drawn to London by the reports of successful brothers of the brush, a school was at last founded which was destined to develop into the glorious English school of painting of the eighteenth century.

The rule of the Protector arrested for a moment this development, but the impulse given was too strong to be permanently stopped, and with the Restoration portrait-painting flourished again with increasing vigour. The men who attained success were still foreigners for the most part, and contented themselves with being weaker reflections of Van Dyck. Sitters demanded portraits in the manner of the master, and no painter had the strength of character to stray from a close and often slavish imitation. The best of them, like Lely and Kneller, both Dutchmen, painted some good portraits but entirely devoid of originality.

There arose, however, about this period a painter, British born, whose strong personality refused to bow down and worship the popular idol, while fully realising his merits. Hogarth dared to look at Nature with his own eyes instead of through Van Dyck's spectacles, and despite opposition insisted on painting things and people as he saw them. He refused to give his models the flattery to which they were accustomed, and his portraits were accordingly not so popular as his conversation pieces. But he had broken the spell: he had proved that it was possible to be a good painter without copying Van Dyck to the letter; and although his realism was not imitated by his successors he secured for them that measure of independence without which no art can attain to greatness.

Such is, briefly, a statement of the history of painting in this country until the middle of the eighteenth century. The remarkable fact appears that until this comparatively late period there is no native school worthy of the name. But about this time there is a complete change, and there arises simultaneously a whole group of men who form a genuinely national school of the greatest brilliancy. British genius asserts itself at last, and for the first time, as a distinct and independent entity, acknowledging its indebtedness to the great masters of the world, but insisting upon its own personal view and temperament. These men accept the lessons of Van Dyck, of Rembrandt, of Raphael, and of Titian; but they say to these noble ancestors: "You are great masters, but Nature is also a great mistress." It is not surprising, then, that side by side with portrait-painting, several will turn their attention to landscape, a branch of painting which hitherto had been completely neglected in this country, and in this branch also they will attain no small measure of success.

PLATE III.—QUEEN CHARLOTTE

Gainsborough painted many portraits of George the Third's consort. The bust here reproduced is in the Victoria and Albert Museum. It is a replica, somewhat less brilliant in colour, of the picture at Windsor Castle.

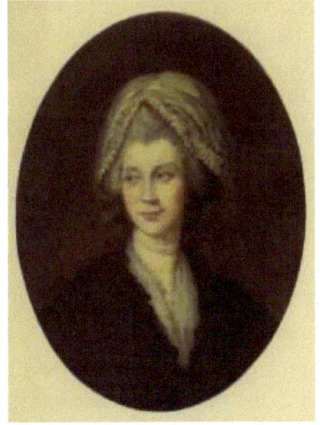

PLATE III.—QUEEN CHARLOTTE

Of all the artists of this golden epoch, which produced such men as Reynolds and Raeburn, Romney, Hoppner, Lawrence, and Turner, the most brilliant and the most versatile was undoubtedly Thomas Gainsborough.

II

GAINSBOROUGH'S EARLY LIFE—IPSWICH AND BATH

Thomas Gainsborough was born at Sudbury in Suffolk in May 1727; he was thus four years younger than Reynolds, thirteen years younger than Wilson. He came from a respectable family of old standing and in comfortable circumstances. His father, John Gainsborough, was a clothier by trade, and of his mother little is known save that she was a gentle and kind woman, very indulgent to her children. They had four daughters and five sons, of whom Thomas was the youngest. Thomas was far from diligent at school; he filled his copy-books with sketches, and was not loth to play the truant in order to get into the woods and meadows, where he would sit drawing trees, flowers, or cattle. A story is even told of his having forged his father's name to a note asking the schoolmaster to "give Tom a holiday." When his father saw the forged note he exclaimed, "The boy will come to be hanged!" but when he was shown the sketches which his son had made during his hours of stolen liberty he changed his verdict to "The boy will be a genius!"

Whatever there may be of truth in this pretty story, a genius Tom turned out to be, and he certainly showed the most remarkable talent when quite a boy. There is a picture by him, painted many years later, the history of which shows that even at this early age he was capable of drawing a man's head rapidly and with great fidelity to the model. The picture is called "Tom Peartree's Portrait," and is a reminiscence of an incident in the painter's childhood. He was sitting one day in his father's garden, concealed by bushes, sketching an old pear tree, when he caught sight of the head of a peasant looking over the wall at the ripe fruit. The expression of eager cupidity in the man's face amused the boy, who included it in his sketch; he afterwards showed it to his father, who recognised the peasant and was able, much to the latter's confusion, to tax him with the intention of stealing his pears.

Such anecdotes serve to show the artist's extraordinary facility with his pencil even as a child, when he had as yet had no training or tuition of any kind. The same valuable quality is evidenced in the works of his maturity, by the marvellous freedom of his technique, and the brilliancy of his brushwork.

His father showed no opposition to his obvious vocation, and at the age of fourteen sent him to London to study painting. It is uncertain whether he went direct to the studio of Hayman, or whether he worked first for a while with Gravelot. Hayman was a portrait-painter of ability, a companion and to some extent an imitator of Hogarth; with him young Gainsborough learned the rudiments of his art, the use of brush and colours, and the principles of composition; but Hayman could teach him little more, and after staying with him four years he returned to Sudbury. It was not long after his return home that he got married, an event which is amusingly related by Cunningham:

"It happened, in one of his pictorial excursions amongst the woods of Suffolk, that he sat down to make a sketch of some fine trees, with sheep reposing below, and some wood-doves roosting above, when a young woman entered unexpectedly upon the scene, and was at once admitted into the landscape and the feelings of the artist. The name of this young lady was Margaret Burr; she was of Scottish extraction and in her sixteenth year, and to the charms of good sense and good looks she added a clear annuity of two hundred pounds. These are matters which no writer of romance would overlook, and were accordingly felt by a young, an ardent, and susceptible man: nor must I omit to tell that country rumour conferred other attractions—she was said to be the natural daughter of one of our exiled princes; nor was she when a wife and a mother desirous of having this circumstance forgotten. On an occasion of household festivity, when her husband was high in fame, she vindicated some little ostentation in her dress by whispering to her niece, now Mrs. Lane, 'I have some right to this; for you know, my love, I am a prince's daughter.' Prince's daughter or not she was wooed and won by Gainsborough, and made him a kind, a prudent, and a submissive wife. The courtship was short. The young pair left Sudbury, leased a small house at a rent of six pounds a year in Ipswich, and making themselves happy in mutual love, conceived they were settled for life."

It was at Ipswich, and not long after his arrival there, that Gainsborough made the acquaintance of Philip Thicknesse, then Governor of Landguard Fort, a man who was to exercise considerable influence upon the artist's life, and to whom we owe much information concerning him. Thicknesse, although he afterwards quarrelled with the painter, and slandered him in a venomous pamphlet, was at first a highly useful friend and not ungenerous patron. Upon his commission Gainsborough painted what was probably his first important landscape; it was a view of Landguard Fort, with figures and sheep in the foreground, and the sea, with the estuary of the Stour, in the distance. This picture was unfortunately destroyed through being hung upon a wall built with mortar mixed with sea water; but we have an excellent engraving of it by Major, and this shows the original to have been a very fine composition. As remuneration Thicknesse gave the artist thirty guineas, and lent him a violin upon which Gainsborough soon acquired considerable proficiency. He retained through life the taste for music of which we find in this incident the first evidence; indeed he seems to have been at least as proud of his achievements in this direction as he was of the creations of his magic brush.

Through the protection of Thicknesse Gainsborough had at this time no lack of commissions for both landscapes and portraits. Of the latter, the most important is that of Admiral Vernon in the National Portrait Gallery, in which the red coat is painted with extreme care. To this period belongs the Miss Hippisley, in the collection of Sir Edward Tennant, and also the heads of his two daughters in the Forster collection at South Kensington Museum.

PLATE IV.—THE BLUE BOY

This world-famous picture, which belongs to the Duke of Westminster, at Grosvenor House, is a portrait of Jonathan Buttall—the son of a wealthy ironmonger who lived in London at the corner of King Street and Greek Street, Soho—in "Van Dyck" costume.

Probably painted at Bath about 1772.

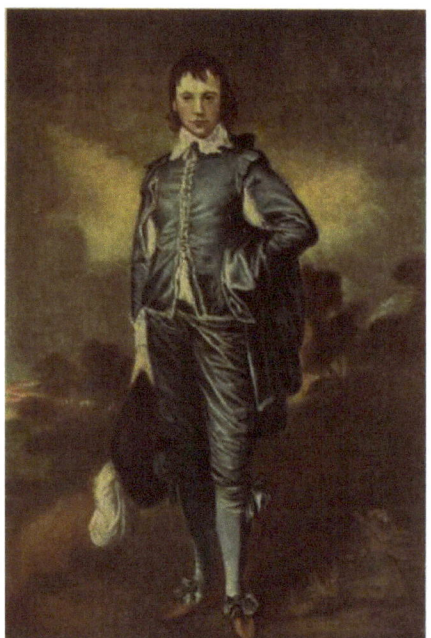

PLATE IV.—THE BLUE BOY

Most of Gainsborough's biographers have treated Thicknesse with but scant justice. No doubt he was a self-satisfied and overbearing man, who had the failing of wishing to manage the lives of those who came into contact with him, and who was equally prompt to take offence, and to offend in retaliation those who would not be led by his dictatorial advice. But in the case of Gainsborough, he certainly rendered him the most inappreciable services, and in the quarrel that followed the artist was probably almost as much to blame as the patron. Be that as it may, it was on Thicknesse's initiative, and on his initiative alone, that Gainsborough removed from Ipswich to Bath in the year 1758. The importance of this move cannot be overrated, and posterity, no less than the painter himself, owes to Philip Thicknesse a considerable debt of gratitude for having been instrumental in bringing it to pass. The horizon at Ipswich was strictly limited; and although no doubt Gainsborough's genius was inborn, he would probably, had he remained in Suffolk, never have developed into the superb painter who must ever be one of the most dazzling stars of the artistic universe. We shall have occasion later to return to this change of scene and to its influence on Gainsborough's life-work.

It was Thicknesse then who persuaded Gainsborough to leave Ipswich and to settle at Bath. Much to the terror of frugal Mrs. Gainsborough, the painter, still acting on his patron's guidance, took a house in the Circus at the annual rental of £50. Thicknesse had many friends at Bath, and to them he warmly recommended his protégé. Whether it was through the influence of Thicknesse, or by the sole force of the artist's own genius, success was soon forthcoming and sitters flocked to his studio. His previous charge of five guineas for a half-length portrait was almost immediately raised to eight, and before very long his patrons became so numerous that he was able to demand no less than forty guineas for a half-length, and one hundred guineas for a full-length, very high prices for those days.

During his stay at Bath Gainsborough devoted much of his time and energy to music; he acquired many musical instruments of various kinds, and tried his hand at all of them. The viol da gamba was apparently his favourite, and in one of his letters to his friend Jackson of Exeter he mentions that he possesses five of these instruments. He heard Giardini, the then unrivalled violinist, and had no rest till he purchased the very instrument that the Italian played on, "but," says Jackson, "seemed much surprised that the music remained with Giardini." In the same way he acquired Abel's viol da gamba; having heard Fischer, he bought a hautboy, then suddenly developed enthusiasm for the harp, and thus passing from instrument to instrument he never had the perseverance to play any one of them with any degree of perfection. In this connection Jackson relates an amusing anecdote of one of his most extravagant acquisitions: "Upon seeing a theorbo in a picture of Van Dyck's he concluded (perhaps because it was finely painted) that the theorbo must be a fine instrument. He recollected to have heard of a German professor, and ascending *per varios gradus* to his garret, found him there at dinner upon a roasted apple, and smoking a pipe.

'I am come,' says he, 'to buy your lute. Come, name your price, and here is your money.'

'I cannot shell my lude!'

'No; not for a guinea or two, but by G— you must sell it.'

'My lude ish wert much monnay! It ish wert ten guineas.'

'That it is. See, here is the money!'

'Well, if I musht; but you will not take it away yourself!'

'Yes, yes. Good-bye——'

(After he had gone down he came up again.)

'I have done but half my errand. What is your lute worth if I have not your book?'

'Whad poog, Maishter Cainsporough?'

'Why, the book of airs you have composed for the lute.'

'Ah, py Cot, I can never part wit my poog!'

PLATE V.—THE HON. MRS. GRAHAM

This portrait of the Hon. Mary Graham (second daughter of Charles, ninth Lord Cathcart) is in the National Gallery of Scotland. Another portrait of the same lady shown in the dress of a housemaid, standing in a doorway with a broom, is supposed to be a rejected design for this picture, and is in the collection of the Earl of Carlisle. Her husband afterwards became Lord Lynedoch.

This picture was painted in 1775-1776, was locked up in a London store for fifty years, but fortunately recovered.

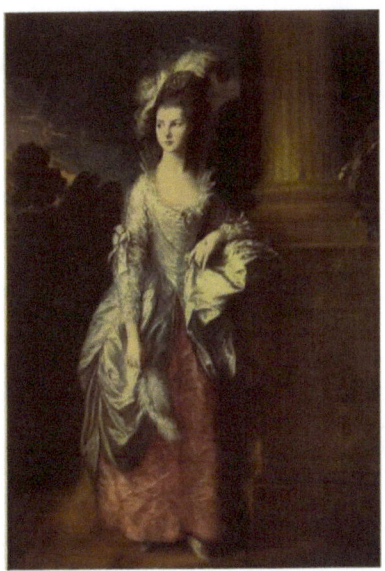

PLATE V.—THE HON. MRS. GRAHAM

'Pooh! you can make another at any time. This is the book I mean' (putting it in his pocket).

'Ah, py Cot, I cannot!'

'Come, come; here's another ten guineas for your book. So, once more good-day t'ye.' (Descends again; and again comes up.) 'But what use is your book to me if I don't understand it? And your lute—you may take it again if you won't teach me to play on it. Come home with me and give me my first lesson.'

'I will come to-morrow.'

'You must come now.'

'I musht tress myshelf.'

'For what? You are the best figure I have seen to-day.'

'I musht be shave.'

'I honour your beard!'

'I musht bud on my wick.'

'D—n your wig! Your cap and beard become you. Do you think if Van Dyck was to paint you he'd let you be shaved?'

"In this way he frittered away his musical talents, and though possessed of ear, taste, and genius, he never had application enough to learn his notes. He seemed to take the first step, the second was, of course, out of his reach, and the summit became unattainable."

Gainsborough made many friends in Bath; mention has already been made of William Jackson of Exeter, with whom he was in constant correspondence, and many of the letters that passed between them are still in existence. He became friendly with David Garrick, whose portrait he painted several times, and another actor with whom he was on very intimate terms was John Henderson. He remained at Bath sixteen years, and it was probably his quarrel with Thicknesse which induced him to migrate once more in 1774.

The true circumstances of his breaking with his earliest patron are not easy to unravel; as is usual in such cases there are two sides to the story, and the truth probably lies somewhere between the two. One fact stands out clearly, namely, that there never was any considerable friendship between Thicknesse and Mrs. Gainsborough; each was probably jealous of the other's ascendency over the artist, and the Governor in his account of their differences makes her appear as the instigator of Gainsborough's behaviour towards himself, and lays practically all the responsibility at her door.

It seems that shortly after the Gainsboroughs settled in Bath a full-length portrait of Miss Ford, who afterwards became Thicknesse's second wife, was painted and presented to that gentleman. All the trouble arose through his desire to possess his own portrait as a companion to that of his wife. We have already seen what a mania Gainsborough had for the viol da gamba; Mrs. Thicknesse had a very fine instrument, "made in the year 1612, of exquisite workmanship and mellifluous tone, and which was certainly worth a hundred guineas." This instrument Gainsborough coveted, and many a time he offered that price for it. "One night," Thicknesse relates, "we asked him and his family to supper with us, after which Mrs. Thicknesse, putting the instrument before him, desired he would play one of his best lessons upon it; this, I say, was after supper, for till poor Gainsborough had got a little borrowed courage (such was his natural modesty), he could neither play nor sing! He then played, and charmingly too, one of his dear friend Abel's lessons, and Mrs. Thicknesse told him he deserved the instrument for his reward, and desired his acceptance of it, but said, 'At your leisure give me my husband's picture to hang by the side of my own.'" Gainsborough was transported with delight and readily agreed. The very next day he began the portrait, finished the head, put in a Newfoundland dog at the sitter's feet, and roughly sketched in the remainder of the picture. There, however, he stopped, and never touched it again; requests, prayers, and remonstrances were in vain, and one day in a fit of temper Gainsborough sent back the viol da gamba to Mrs. Thicknesse, and shortly afterwards also sent the unfinished picture just as it was. At this Thicknesse was of course much offended. "Every time," he says, "I went into the room where that scarecrow hung it gave me so painful a sensation that I protest it often turned me sick, and in one of those sick fits I desired Mrs. Thicknesse would return the picture to Mr. Gainsborough. This she consented to do, provided I would permit her to send with it a card, expressing her sentiments at the same time, to which I am sorry to say I too hastily consented. In that card she bid him take his brush, and first rub out the countenance of the truest and warmest friend he ever had, and so done, then blot him for ever from his memory."

Such is Thicknesse's own story of the quarrel, but according to Allan Cunningham, Gainsborough did actually, without her husband's knowledge, give Mrs. Thicknesse a hundred guineas for the viol da gamba, and then did not consider it incumbent upon him to pay twice over by painting the portrait. This is, however, hardly a plausible tale and the probabilities are that Thicknesse's version is nearer the truth. However that may be the long friendship between the artist and his protector came to an end, and Gainsborough having taken a dislike to Bath removed to London.

III

GAINSBOROUGH'S LIFE IN LONDON—LAST YEARS AND DEATH

Gainsborough was forty-seven years of age when he came to settle definitely in London; his genius had reached the highest point of its development. This new change of scene, great and important though it was, cannot be looked upon as being by any means so risky an experiment as his move from Ipswich to Bath. He had by this time a firmly established connection, and it must not be forgotten that in those days Bath was a highly fashionable watering-place, bearing to London very much the same relation as the French Riviera does at the present time. Everybody who was anybody socially in the capital was a more or less frequent visitor to Bath, and Gainsborough during his stay there had ample opportunities to make acquaintances which were bound to stand him in good stead when he came to London. Thicknesse, however, even after their quarrel, could not refrain from sending him forth once more under his particular patronage; he wrote to Lord Bateman, a peer of little influence or importance, asking him "for both our sakes to give him countenance and make him known, that being all which is necessary." This sort of thing was probably quite superfluous, for Gainsborough was by this time fully capable of holding his own even in London. Still it remains on record that Lord Bateman did do his best for him, and himself acquired several of his pictures.

On their first arrival in London the Gainsboroughs took quarters north of the Oxford Road; a more central and more fashionable neighbourhood was, however, necessary to the painter, and he very soon removed to Schomberg House in Pall Mall. This house, which was built by the Duke of Schomberg towards the end of the seventeenth century, was at this time the property of the eccentric and mediocre painter John Astley, a fellow pupil with Reynolds under Hudson. From Astley Gainsborough rented a third of the house at £300 a year, showing that he had from the first no anxiety as to his success in the metropolis. An interesting circumstance in relation to this house is that some seven years later another portion of it was occupied by the quack Dr. Graham, who installed there his Temple of Health. In some of the strange and not very legitimate ceremonies carried on in this "Temple," the part of goddess of health was played by none other than Emma Lyon or Hart, who was destined to become so famous as the lovely Lady Hamilton. Gainsborough must have met her, and although we have no actual portrait from his hand of this wonderfully beautiful creature, it is suggested by Sir Walter Armstrong that she may have sat for the picture of "Musidora" in the National Gallery, one of the very rare attempts at the nude which Gainsborough is known to have made.

PLATE VI.—THE DUCHESS OF DEVONSHIRE
(In the collection of Earl Spencer, K.G.)

This delightful painting, one of the gems of the Althorp collection, is considered to be one of the master's greatest achievements in full-length portraits.

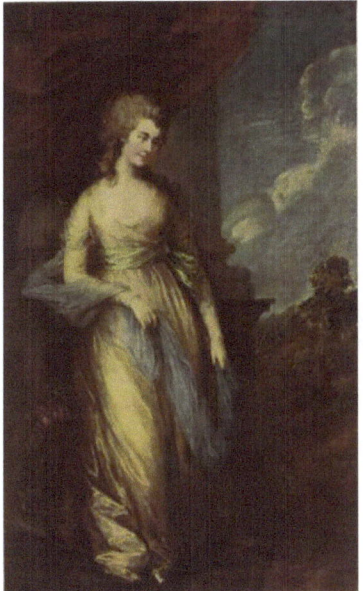

PLATE VI.—THE DUCHESS OF DEVONSHIRE

In London Gainsborough came into personal contact with Sir Joshua Reynolds, probably for the first time, although from a note of Walpole in his catalogue of the Royal Academy of 1773 it would appear that they had been in touch with one another some years previously, Walpole's words being: "Gainsborough and Dance, having disagreed with Sir Joshua Reynolds, did not send any pictures to this exhibition." When the Academy was founded in 1768 Gainsborough was one of the original members, and to the first four exhibitions he sent from Bath seventeen portraits and fifteen landscapes. Then for four years, no doubt on account of the disagreement mentioned by Walpole, he exhibited nothing until 1777, when his name reappears in the catalogue with portraits of the Duke and Duchess of Cumberland.

The vogue of Gainsborough was now at its height, and a long series of portraits of royal personages began to occupy his easel. It was one of these which, a few years later, led to his final quarrel with the Royal Academy. To the exhibition of 1783 he had sent eight portraits and portrait groups, including one of the three "Eldest Princesses." He sent the frames only in the first instance, but kept back that of the princesses, the king and queen having expressed a wish to view the picture before it was sent to the Academy. There was then a rule of the exhibition, one which is still in force, that full-length portraits could not be hung on the line, and by some misapprehension, it must have been thought by the hanging committee that this was a full-length group. Gainsborough must have heard of the place which had been assigned to it, and he sent the following curt note to Somerset House, where the Royal Academy exhibitions were then held:—

"Mr. Gainsborough presents his Compliments to the Gentlemen appointed to hang the pictures at the Royal Academy, and begs leave to hint *to them that if the Royal Family, which he has sent for this Exhibition (being smaller than three-quarters), are hung above the line along with full-lengths, he never more, whilst he breathes, will send another Picture to the Exhibition.*

This he swears by God.

Saturday morn."

This letter did not have the desired effect, so Gainsborough withdrew his pictures and never exhibited again. It would appear that such a quarrel, obviously the result of a misunderstanding, could easily have been adjusted by the President, had he felt inclined to interfere; but Sir Joshua evidently preferred to let matters take their course, and so the break became permanent.

There never was any great sympathy between the two men, although their mutual admiration for each other's work was considerable. Their characters were essentially different, and although they frequently shared the same sitters, and had some friends in common, they lived in a social atmosphere entirely distinct. On the other hand they never were enemies, nor had any serious personal quarrel; at one time it even seemed as though they might be drawn into friendship, and Gainsborough started painting the President's portrait; this, however, shared the fate of Thicknesse's years before and got no further than the first sitting. Their relations were such, however, that Gainsborough was able to call Reynolds to his death-bed, although they had probably had no intercourse for years. The pathetic story of Gainsborough's last illness is best told in the words of Allan Cunningham: "Though Gainsborough was not partial to the society of literary men, he seems to have been acquainted with Johnson and with Burke, and he lived on terms of great affection with Richard Brinsley Sheridan. He was also a welcome visitor at the table of Sir George Beaumont, a gentleman of graceful manners, who lived in old English dignity, and was, besides, a lover of literature and a painter of landscape. The latter loved to relate a curious anecdote of Gainsborough, which marks the unequal spirit of the man, and shows that he was the slave of wayward impulses which he could neither repress nor command. Sir George Beaumont, Sheridan, and Gainsborough had dined together, and the latter was more than usually pleasant and witty. The meeting was so much to their mutual satisfaction that they agreed to have another day's happiness, and accordingly an early day was named when they should dine again together. They met, but a cloud had descended upon the spirit of Gainsborough, and he sat silent with a look of fixed melancholy, which no wit could dissipate. At length he took Sheridan by the hand, led him out of the room, and said, "Now, don't laugh, but listen. I shall die soon—I know it—I feel it. I have less time to live than my looks infer; but for this I care not. What oppresses my mind is this: I have many acquaintances and few friends; and as I wish to have one worthy man to accompany me to the grave, I am desirous of bespeaking you. Will you come; aye or no?" Sheridan could scarcely repress a smile as he made the required promise; the looks of Gainsborough cleared up like the sunshine of one of his own landscapes; throughout the rest of the evening his wit flowed and his humour ran over, and the minutes, like those of the poet, winged their way with pleasure.

About a year after the promise obtained from Sheridan to attend his funeral he went to hear the impeachment of Warren Hastings, and, sitting with his back to an open window, suddenly felt something inconceivably cold touch his neck above the shirt collar. It was accompanied with stiffness and pain. On returning home he mentioned what he felt to his wife and his niece, and on looking they saw a mark about the size of a shilling, which was harder to the touch than the surrounding skin, and which he said still felt cold. The application of flannel did not remove it, and the artist becoming alarmed, consulted one after the other the most eminent surgeons of London—John Hunter himself the last. They all declared there was no danger; but there was that presentiment upon Gainsborough from which none perhaps escape. He laid his hand repeatedly on his neck and said to his sister, who had hastened to London to see him, "If this be a cancer, I am a dead man." And a cancer it proved to be. When this cruel disease fairly discovered itself, it was found to be inextricably interwoven with the threads of life, and he prepared himself for death with cheerfulness and perfect composure. He desired to be buried near his friend Kirby in Kew churchyard, and that his name only should be cut on his grave-stone. He sent for Reynolds, and peace was made between them. Gainsborough exclaimed to Sir Joshua: "We are all going to heaven, and Van Dyck is of the company," and immediately expired—August 2nd, 1788, in the sixty-first year of his age. Sheridan and the president attended him to the grave.

PLATE VII.—MRS. ROBINSON—"Perdita"

(At the Wallace Collection)

This portrait of the beautiful actress is one of Gainsborough's finest masterpieces. The lightness, dexterity, and transparency of the pigment is almost unrivalled, not only in this artist's work, but in any picture of the eighteenth century. It hangs in the Wallace Collection at Hertford House; a smaller sketch of the same subject is at Windsor Castle.

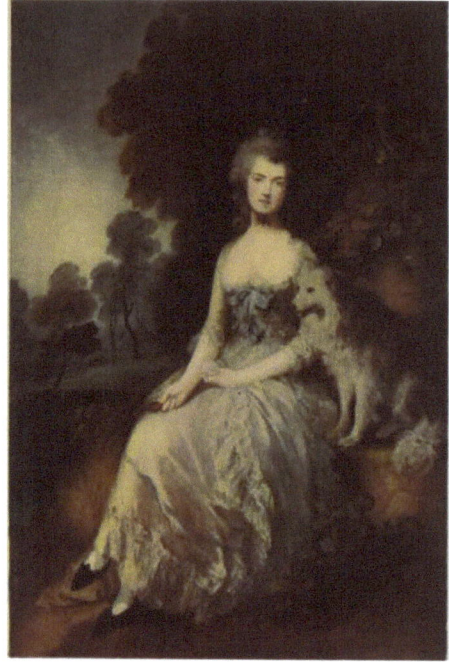

PLATE VII.—MRS. ROBINSON—"Perdita"

Gainsborough left two daughters, whose portraits he painted several times. The elder one, Margaret, did not marry; while the younger, Mary, was secretly wedded in 1780 to her father's friend, Johann Christian Fischer, the hautboy player. This marriage caused Gainsborough much trouble; he foresaw that the musician's irritability and eccentric behaviour on many occasions could not conduce to the happiness of his daughter; however, to quote his own letter to his sister, Mrs. Gibbon, "As it was too late for me to alter anything without being the cause of total unhappiness on both sides, my *consent*, which was a mere compliment to affect to ask, I needs must give." The father's foreboding was only too fully justified; the union turned out very unhappy from the first, and within a year or so husband and wife separated. Both sisters were mentally deficient, and their aberrations increased with age to the point of total derangement. Mary, soon after her marriage, became subject to wild hallucinations, "perhaps the most reasonable" (as Fulcher puts it) being that the Prince of Wales was pursuing her with his love. After her mother's death she went to live with her sister, whose mental condition was even worse than her own; they would receive no visitors who did not belong to the nobility, so that many who wished to gain admittance to the house were obliged to assume titles which they did not possess. Margaret died about 1824, and Mary a year or two later; before her death she insisted on presenting to the king the portrait of Fischer, painted by her father at Bath about forty years before; this portrait is now in the Royal Collection.

Of Gainsborough's personality and character much has no doubt been gathered from the preceding pages. His physical appearance is familiar from his own portraits of himself, and from that which Zoffany painted of him. He was handsome, tall and strong, with large features and a broad if not very high forehead; the small eyes are quick and observant, the mouth sensitive and rather undecided. In the choice of his friends he attached little importance to breeding and none to social position; he was generous and open-handed to all, with money to his relations and often indiscriminately with his works to friends or mere acquaintances: on one occasion he gave his picture of the "Boy at the Stile" to Colonel Hamilton (equally well known at the time as an amateur violinist and a gentleman pugilist) for having played him a solo on the violin; to Wiltshire, the carrier who took his pictures from Bath to London, and who refused to take payment in money from the artist, he presented many valuable landscapes.

Intellectually he was extremely gifted; although his education in his youth was much neglected his letters show him to have been by no means ignorant or uncultivated. They also bear the impress of his spontaneous wit and keen humour; of this quality there is evidence in numerous anecdotes. An old man of the labouring class, named Fowler, used to sit to him at Bath; on the studio mantelpiece stood a child's skull, the gift of a medical friend.

"Fowler, without moving his position, continually peered at it askance, with inquisitive eye. 'Ah! Master Fowler,' said the painter, 'that is a mighty curiosity.' 'What might it be, sir, if I may make so bold?' 'A whale's eye,' was the grave reply. 'No, no, never say so, Muster Gainsborough. Sir, it is a little child's skull!' 'You have hit it,' said the wag. 'Why, Fowler, you're a witch! But what will you say when I tell you it is the skull of Julius Cæsar when he was a little boy!' 'Laws!' cried Fowler, 'what a phenomenon!'"

Gainsborough's temper was very hasty, quite opposed to the patient courtliness of Reynolds. When a certain peer or alderman, posing, with boundless self-satisfaction, for his portrait, begged the artist not to overlook the dimple in his chin, "Damn the dimple in your chin, I will paint neither the one nor the other!" was the uncompromising rejoinder.

These stories, unimportant as they are, serve to give an insight into the man's character; but whatever his personal faults and qualities may or may not have been it is with his works that posterity is chiefly concerned, and by them and them alone that Gainsborough must be judged.

GAINSBOROUGH'S WORKS

The works of Gainsborough may be divided into three chronological groups, just as his life was divided between three distinct localities. But whereas there is a definite and fundamental difference between the pictures painted at Ipswich and those of the remainder of his life, there is not to any similar extent a determined demarkation between his productions at Bath and those of his last and most glorious years in London.

It has been seen that Gainsborough used palette and brush from at least the age of fourteen, when he went to London to study with Hayman. But the productions of this very early period are extremely difficult to identify. The National Gallery of Ireland possesses two drawings in pencil, portraits of a man and a woman, on each of which appears the signature *Tho: Gainsborough fecit 1743-1744*. These, the earliest extant attempts of Gainsborough in portraiture are hard and laboured in execution, but the heads are well-modelled and full of character; they must have been done in London before his return to his native Sudbury.

A similar hardness and elaborate care and attention to detail characterises the early landscapes painted in Suffolk. The only pictures of the old masters to which the young artist could have had access at this period were landscapes of Dutch painters such as Ruysdael, Hobbema, and Wynants. Their influence is obvious in his own early productions, especially that of Wynants; the most important work of this character is the large landscape belonging to Mr. J. D. Cobbold of Ipswich; it is an elaborate composition, semi-classical in style, with conventional hills in the distance, and a carefully put in group of cattle and figures in the foreground. This is the sort of thing that Thicknesse must have found in the painter's studio upon his first visit, together with the portrait of Admiral Vernon (now in the National Portrait Gallery), and others which the Governor describes as "truly drawn, perfectly like, but stiffly painted and worse coloured."

The "Landguard Fort" was commissioned by Thicknesse shortly after the artist's marriage and removal to Ipswich, and must therefore have been painted between 1747 and 1750; it thus establishes an important landmark in the painter's early years, and although the original is unfortunately lost, it is possible from the engraving of it, which still exists, to approximately date other early landscapes of Gainsborough. To about the same time probably belongs the "View in Suffolk" of the Irish National Gallery, while the "Cornard Wood" in the National Gallery, somewhat more free in execution, is slightly later.

Of the portraits of this period very few can be traced, and it is probable that no large number were painted. The "Admiral Vernon" has already been mentioned and also the

"Miss Hippisley" (Sir Edward Tennant's collection), and the heads of the artist's daughters at South Kensington. There are also in existence two half-length ovals of Mr. Robert Edgar and Miss Katherine Edgar, the latter probably one of the best examples of Gainsborough's later years in Suffolk. They all show the same characteristic tightness, and a lack of that marvellous freedom for which his later works are so remarkable.

PLATE VIII.—MISS HAVERFIELD

(At the Wallace Collection)

Portraits of children by Gainsborough are not frequent, although he introduced country boys and lasses into his landscapes with the greatest success. This example in the Wallace Collection possesses a charm which makes one regret that his youthful sitters were not more numerous.

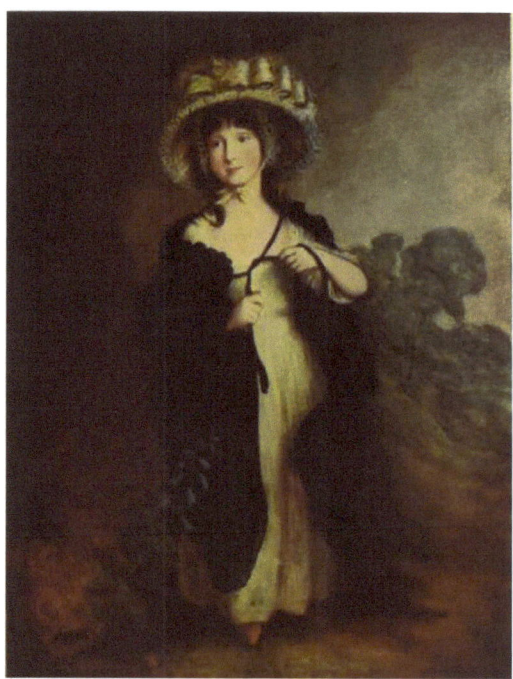

PLATE VIII.—MISS HAVERFIELD

Almost directly after his settlement at Bath the artist's manner changed very appreciably. This was probably due chiefly to the fact that he was able in the neighbourhood of Bath to see and study the works of great masters of the past, and notably the great family group by Van Dyck at Wilton House. He no doubt also had access to the fine array of works by Rubens then hanging at Blenheim and unfortunately now dispersed. The paintings of these masters seem to have disclosed to Gainsborough the possibilities of his materials, and from this moment his artistic development is rapid and decided, much more rapid than is generally believed. Most people imagine that all his best works date from the years of his life in London after 1774, and that the pictures of his Bath period, previous to that year, are comparatively much inferior. This is quite a mistake, for many of his most famous works were in fact painted at Bath and his genius had reached its full maturity long before he settled in Pall Mall. The fine half-length of Miss Linley and her brother, belonging to Lord Sackville at Knole, Lord Burton's "Lady Sussex and Lady Barbara Yelverton," the large equestrian portrait of General Honywood, several portraits of Garrick, such landscapes as those belonging to Lord Tweedmouth, Lord Bateman, and Mr. Lionel Phillipps were all painted at Bath, as was probably also the immortal "Blue Boy" itself.

One of the first of Gainsborough's sitters after his arrival at Bath was Mr. Robert Craggs Nugent, afterwards Viscount Clare and Earl Nugent, whose full-length portrait was the first picture ever sent by the artist to a public exhibition. It was shown at the Spring Garden Exhibition of the Society of Artists of Great Britain in 1761 and now belongs to Sir George Nugent. In the following year a picture entered in the Society's catalogue as "A whole-length portrait of a gentleman with a gun," has been identified as the picture, now at Althorp, of William Poyntz, brother of Georgiana, the first Countess Spencer, herself the mother of that more famous Georgiana, Duchess of Devonshire. Both the mother and the daughter were painted about the same time, the latter as a little girl of five or six years of age. These two pictures of the usual half-length size are also at Althorp.

Year by year Gainsborough continued sending portraits and landscapes to the Society's exhibitions, the huge canvas of General Honywood on horseback hanging there in 1765; the next year came, among others, the full-length portrait of Garrick leaning against a bust of Shakespeare,painted for the Town Hall, Stratford-on-Avon, where it still hangs.

In 1769 the Royal Academy opened its first exhibition; Gainsborough was represented by four pictures, including a whole-length portrait of Isabella, Lady Molyneux, afterwards Countess of Sefton, and another of George Pitt, first Lord Rivers. In 1770 we find six pictures and a book of drawings, in the following year five full-lengths and two landscapes, and in 1772 no less than fourteen pictures, four of which were portraits, and ten "drawings in imitation of oil-painting;" these latter, of which a few exist, are curious productions drawn in water-colour on thick coarse paper laid down on canvas and then varnished; the process is not a very happy one, and the artist's fancy for it does not appear to have been lasting.

For the four following years Gainsborough's name is absent from the Academy catalogues from the cause already mentioned of a disagreement with Reynolds as recorded by Walpole. But during this time Gainsborough no doubt continued to turn out "heads" in great numbers, and not a few full-lengths, to say nothing of landscapes of varying size and importance. Several of these half-lengths are in the National Portrait Gallery and the National Gallery, while a considerable number are to be found in private collections.

Sir Walter Armstrong, in his monumental work on Gainsborough, puts forward very forcibly the theory that the famous "Blue Boy" at Grosvenor House was painted about the year 1770 at Bath and not in 1779 in London, as has been generally supposed. It is impossible to reproduce here his closely reasoned arguments, but his conclusion is most probably correct that the "Blue Boy" is a masterpiece of Gainsborough's "Bath period." It is a portrait of a certain Jonathan Buttall, a very wealthy ironmonger who lived at the corner of King Street and Greek Street, Soho. He is represented at full-length, standing in a landscape, in a rich blue "Van Dyck" costume, holding a large hat with a white feather in his right hand. The history of the picture and the manner of its coming into the possession of the Duke of Westminster are uncertain; it may have been sold together with the effects of Jonathan Buttall, senior, after the death of his widow in 1796, when all his property was disposed of by public auction. It seems to have belonged to Hoppner, who died in 1810, and who probably is the author of the very good copy of the "Blue Boy" which is now in America, and has sometimes been looked upon as a replica from the master's own hand.

To this same period in the artist's career probably belongs another and almost equally famous picture which hangs on the same walls as the "Blue Boy." The Duke of Westminster's "Cottage Door," one of the finest of Gainsborough's landscapes or pastoral scenes, appears to have been a product of the last years spent at Bath, together with the great "Watering Place" at the National Gallery; the "Rustic Children" belonging to Lord Carnarvon and of which a small version is also in the National collection; Mr. G. L. Basset's "Cottage Girl," and many other landscapes of equal or lesser importance.

It is therefore fair to surmise that had Gainsborough never made his last move from Bath to London the world's stock of artistic treasures would in all probability not have been very much the poorer. That he did afterwards create works of greater beauty was presumably not the effect of his settlement in the metropolis, but merely of the continuance of the natural development of his genius; to the very end of his career he continued to profit by the lessons of greater experience; his touch constantly grew more free, more feathery, his pigment more transparent, his insight into character more rapid and more sure. The increased elegance and heightened refinement of his later portraits may or may not be due to a closer touch with the court and its immediate surroundings; but, from what has gone before, it is clear that it is a delusion to speak deprecatingly of a "Gainsborough of the Bath period."

It is by no means easy to assign dates to most of the pictures painted by Gainsborough in London. The Academy catalogues provide but slight assistance; for one thing portraits were almost invariably unnamed in those days and can only be identified in most cases by the help of contemporary criticism or correspondence; besides, as we have seen, Gainsborough's first reappearance at the official exhibition took place in 1777 with the portraits of the Duke and Duchess of Cumberland, and his final quarrel with the institution was only a few years later. But the beautiful women and men of fashion who sat to him were legion. Portraits such as that of "Mrs. Robinson" in the Wallace Collection, "Mrs. Siddons" in the National Gallery, "The Hon. Mrs. Graham" in the Scottish National Gallery are too well known and too easily accessible to need description. Many, however, of his greatest works are hidden away from the general public in private collections, and only reveal themselves now and again when their owners consent to lend them to an exhibition.

Among these is Lord Rothschild's "The Morning Walk," which may perhaps be looked upon as Gainsborough's most perfect masterpiece. It is a portrait group of Squire Hallett and his wife walking in a landscape with a white Pomeranian dog. As in many of the master's finest achievements the colour-scheme is of the soberest description; like the "Lady Mulgrave" or Lord Normanton's marvellous "Lady Mendip" it is almost a monochrome. Yet, by a sort of magic, such pictures as these give the impression of a superb melody of colour; every touch conduces to a most perfect harmony, and the effect is obtained by a method so personal, so entirely new to his time, that Reynolds, speaking of him in one of his discourses, was able to say that "his handling, the manner of leaving the colours, ... had very much the appearance of the work of an artist who had never learned from others the usual and regular practice belonging to his art."

And indeed a survey of Gainsborough's life-work leads one to agree with the words of Sir Joshua, but in a wider sense than the President intended them to apply. Gainsborough owed little or nothing to the great masters of painting who came before him, and less to any of his contemporaries. His teachers were Nature and his own sympathy with his subject. Nowhere in the work of his maturity is there to be found any trace of imitation of the Dutch or of the Italian masters. He did not pose his models *à la* Van Dyck, nor did he borrow his palette from Titian; he is the most English of English artists as he is the greatest glory of English art. "He is an immortal painter," says Ruskin, "and his excellence is based on principles of art long acknowledged and facts of Nature universally apparent."